MOM!!! REALLY???

*A Faith-Based Guide for Parents to
Knock Down Barriers Preventing Healthy
Communication Within the Household*

Be Free Enterprises, LLC
341 S 3rd Street
Suite 100-264
Columbus, OH 43215

Unless otherwise noted, Scripture quotations identified as KJV are

from the King James Version.

Editor: Joylynn M. Ross

Cover Design: Robles Designs

ISBN: 978-1-7328442-0-9

Library of Congress Control Number: 2018913028
Mom!!! Really???/ Candice Simpson
1.Non-Fiction–African American
2. Non-Fiction-Spiritual and Religion
3. Non-Fiction-Self-Help
4. Non-Fiction-Journal

Disclaimer: *This guide is not a substitute for counseling. If you discover that you need additional assistance to process information, please seek professional help and/or counseling.*

Printed in the United States of America

10 9 8 7 6 5 4 3 2 1

MOM!!! REALLY???

A Faith-Based Guide for Parents to Knock Down Barriers
Preventing Healthy Communication Within the Household

Candice P. Simpson

Dedication

I dedicate this book to my father, Rod Simpson Sr., and mother, Viola Hazel Calhoun, for all your sacrifices, support, prayers, and guidance on how to raise my daughter. Your transparency and honesty about your past and how to overcome through Jesus Christ has helped me to grow as an individual and become a better parent. I love you both. Thank you!

Table of Contents

Prayer

Heavenly Father, bless every reader who purchases this guide. As every reader takes an honest assessment of self, allow the Holy Spirit to bring correction, repentance, healing, and deliverance to those areas that are creating barriers in the household, including the parent-child relationship. Give every reader divine instruction on how to repair the breaches so You can get the glory on this earth.

In Jesus' name, Amen.

Introduction

In today's society, it can be very hard for the next generation to form their identity in Christ, especially when the majority of what they see and hear on television, social media, or in music is contrary to what the Word of God says. Several years ago, God revealed to me a prophetic dream, warning me that young people, including my own daughter, were under severe attack by the enemy. This attack takes place when they transition to teenagers and young adults. God revealed that a demonic spirit of confusion and deception was released to destroy and distort their identity, hindering them from walking in the fullness of their purpose and destiny here on this earth.

This revelation caused me to seek God in prayer

and fasting like never before. My purpose was to seek instructions on how to protect the young people. As a result, God revealed that the foundation of communication had been breached within the homes, which led Satan to bring separation in the parent-child relationship. Separation in the parent-child relationship is often created when young people are not comfortable communicating with their parents about how they feel, act, or see in the world around them. This is because the conversations are typically one-sided from the parents' point of view. In learning that this was a major part of the problem, I was then led to not only reveal this problem, but to also share tips and strategies on how to solve it, which is why I wrote this guide.

Parents, including myself, have not effectively communicated nor shown our youth or young adults on a consistent basis that the emotions they are feeling—such as anger, lust, confusion, and hurt—are normal. Instead, we have shamed or condemned our children for not being the "perfect child," which led to Satan entering in and causing rebellion, confusion, identity issues, and unhealthy communication within the household.

In this guide, you will explore barriers as well as strategies to knock down those barriers by assessing, commanding, and creating an atmosphere that is conducive for building healthy communication within the household. At the end of chapters one through three, there will be open-ended questions from a practical and biblical point of view, as well as a reflection section. These questions are to raise the awareness and/or identify any barriers that are preventing healthy communication within the household. Be sure to answer each question with honesty so you can bring correction, unity, and peace to your household.

In chapter four, you will begin to command the atmosphere to be conducive for healthy communication by speaking the Word of God. Commanding your atmosphere means you will speak the Word of God in authority, believing that peace, unity, and love will abide in your house. Chapter five will help you develop a strategic plan of action to create an atmosphere by establishing family activities that promote healthy communication. Creating your atmosphere to promote open communication will close the door to all the enemy tactics.

I encourage you to limit distractions and find some alone time. Also, set aside time before and after each chapter to pray. Have your Bible and pen or pencil available to answer the questions in this guide. Consider having additional notebook paper in case you run out of space provided in this guide, as well as to jot down anything that flows through your spirit.

Chapter 1

Parenting Styles

"Train up a child in the way he should go: and when he is old, he will not depart from it." (Proverbs 22:6).

Growing up, I always heard the following quotes: "Honor thy mother and father and your days will be longer." or "Because I said so!" I was taught to respect and obey my elders no matter what, even if I didn't agree or understand. This type of belief as a child, resulted in me becoming rebellious and angry as I got older because I had no healthy outlet to communicate my thoughts and feelings. If you ask my closest friends or family members, they will tell you I was always on punishment or getting popped in my mouth for talking back to adults.

I have learned during spiritual counseling, reading, and studying God's Word that in order to have or strengthen your communication with your child or children, you must take an honest look at your parenting style. Parenting styles describe the way parents tend to respond or react to their child. Mostly, parenting styles are learned behaviors from childhood; what a parent learned from their own parents. Researchers have identified four types of parenting styles: lenient, uninvolved, strict parenting, and healthy parenting. Let's take a brief look at these four parenting styles.

The Lenient Parent: No Structure and No Boundaries

Have you ever come across children in a restaurant, grocery store, or in a department store who are so unruly and allowed to roam around freely? You look around for the parent to see if they are going to tell them to sit down, only to witness the parent continuing to simply sit there or shop with no regard toward the other people trying to shop or eat and enjoy their meal. If you have, this is what is referred to as a lenient style of parenting. They rarely discipline or set rules, and they tend to allow their children to do whatever they want. Research shows this style of parenting produces children who feel entitled, are disrespectful, and have behavioral problems such as anger outbursts in school, or the inability to interact with people in public places because they are used to having their way. Billy Graham said it best: "A child who is allowed to be disrespectful to his parents will not have true respect for anyone."

The Uninvolved Parent: Neglectful and Emotionally Disconnected

The uninvolved parent may provide the basic essentials (food, housing, and clothing), but struggle to meet the emotional or physical needs of their children. This may be caused by the parent having some type of emotional, financial, or social problem where they are so consumed with self, they can't be there for their child. This type of parenting makes it difficult for children to trust people and teaches them to suppress their emotions, which may lead to depression or other emotional detachment. Researchers have found that those children who feel unimportant and unloved tend to act out in school, have problems with listening to authority figures, and many times struggle with substance abuse to cope with negative emotions to feel "happy." This particular parenting style is easily inherited from one generation to the next, and as the children grow up, they often repeat the same patterns learned.

The Strict Parent: Follow My Rules or Else

This strict parent has severe control issues. This style of parenting sets strict rules for the child to follow. Failure to obey these rules results in harsh punishments. The strict parent displays minimum communication and leaves no room for the child to communicate their thoughts, feelings, or concerns. The strict parent wants "perfect robots" whom they can control. They also require the child to achieve a high level of accomplishments in school, sports, etc. This style of parenting suppresses the child's emotions to the point where they learn unhealthy coping skills that may lead to low self-esteem, unhealthy relationships, and failure to stand up to wrongdoing.

The Healthy Parent: Fair, Firm, and Consistent

The healthy parent is big on establishing balance in the parent-child relationship. This style of parenting has high expectations by creating rules and boundaries, but what separates this type of parenting style from the others is that there is consistency. This allows the child the freedom of expression, and discipline when necessary. These parents tend to be more transparent in their parenting approach by leading by example and sharing their shortcomings for teachable moments. Research have shown that this style of parenting also teaches children how to process emotions, which allows for healthy decision-making.

Understanding the four different parenting styles can help you evaluate what parenting style(s) you are currently operating in, and areas you need to improve upon to have healthy communication. As parents, it should be our goal to operate consistently by being fair, firm, and consistent with our children.

Below you will have the opportunity to take an honest look at your parenting style by answering questions from a practical and biblical approach.

Open-Ended Questions

After having reviewed the four different parenting styles, answer the questions below in the space provided:

1. What parenting style(s) do you resemble the

most?

_____

_____

_____

_____

_____

_____

_____

_____

2. What parenting style(s) did your parents have when you were growing up?

_____

_____

_____

_____

_____

_____

_____

_____

3. Where did your parents learn their style of parenting?

_____

_____

_____

_____

_____

_____

_____

_____

4. Did you adopt all or some of your parents' parenting style?

_____

_____

_____

_____

_____

_____

_____

_____

_____

5. How does it influence your own parenting style?

_____

_____

_____

_____

_____

_____

_____

6. If you were to ask your children about your parenting style, what do you think they would say?

_____

_____

_____

_____

_____

_____

_____

_____

7. What are some barriers that are preventing healthy parenting in your household?

_____

_____

_____

_____

_____

_____

_____

8. What are some strengths you have when parenting your children?

_____

_____

_____

_____

_____

_____

_____

_____

Biblical Questions

God gives His pattern in the Bible for parenting. After reading the accompanying Scripture, answer the questions below in the space provided:

1. What does God say about treating children with respect, love, and kindness? **Ephesians**

6:4; Colossians 3:21; Isaiah 66:13; Psalm 103:13

_____

_____

_____

_____

_____

_____

_____

_____

2. What does God say about teaching children to live as believers? **Proverbs 22:6; Deuteronomy 11:1-32**

_____

_____

_____

_____

_____

_____

_____

_____

_____

3. What does God say about being role models?

   Genesis 18:19; Titus 2:2-15

_____

_____

_____

_____

_____

_____

_____

_____

4. What does God say about being a provider? **2**

   Corinthians 12:14; 1 Timothy 5:8

_____

_____

_____

_____

_____

_____

_____

_____

_____

5. What does God say about guiding the household? **1 Timothy 3: 4-5, 12**

_____

_____

_____

_____

_____

_____

_____

6. What does God say about discipline? **Proverbs**

29: 15, 17

_____

_____

_____

_____

_____

_____

_____

_____

Reflection:

After answering the above questions, take the next 10 minutes to reflect on what you wrote from a practical and biblical viewpoint. This time of reflection is to raise your awareness about any old patterns, beliefs, and mindsets that may have created barriers of unhealthy communication within the household.

After your time of reflection, use the space provided

below to journal about the following questions:

(1) What did you learn overall from the answering the questions: positive and/or negative emotions, thought and feelings?

_____

_____

_____

_____

_____

_____

_____

_____

_____

_____

_____

_____

_____

_____

_____

_____

(2) What parenting style(s) did you most identify
with? Why? Were you surprised?

_____

_____

_____

_____

_____

_____

_____

_____

_____

_____

_____

_____

_____

_____

_____

_____

(3) After learning more about your parenting style(s), do you have to ask for forgiveness from self, parents, children, and/or others? If so, why?

_____

_____

_____

_____

_____

_____

_____

_____

_____

_____

_____

_____

_____

_____

_____

(4) How can the Word of God assist you in making

changes?

_____

_____

_____

_____

_____

_____

_____

_____

_____

_____

_____

_____

_____

_____

_____

_____

(5) What strengths do you have that you can continue to implement as a healthy parent on a consistent basis?

_____

_____

_____

_____

_____

_____

_____

_____

_____

_____

_____

_____

_____

_____

_____

_____

_____

Chapter 2

Communication Styles

"And, ye fathers, provoke not your children to wrath; but bring them up in the nurture and admonition of the Lord" (*Ephesians 6:4*).

As I mentioned in the last chapter, I had to go through spiritual counseling, reading, and applying the Word of God to deal with old belief systems that hindered me from effectively communicating with my daughter. One of the belief systems, which is a continuing dying process for me, is the old saying "children should be seen and not heard" (or listened to), which can definitely lead to a one-sided conversation. This belief system affected me hard as I transitioned into adolescence. It prevented me from being able to speak with my parents about my thoughts and feelings, as well as process them in a healthy manner. It resulted in me making poor decisions early on in life that I still have to deal with today.

The way parents communicate with their children can build or tear down, and even shape how they communicate with others. I can recall asking my daughter and her friends why they find it hard to communicate with their parents. They shared the following: "They wouldn't understand," "They don't listen," "We have to be this perfect Christian and we don't want to let them down," and "We don't want them worrying about us all the time and controlling us."

Listening to their opinions without judgement or giving a lecture opened the door for my daughter and her friends to become more open and honest about their feelings, which in turn benefited me, because I was able to learn their inner thoughts and develop better ways to communicate.

When communicating with my daughter, I learned that I had to be intentional with active listening and responding out of love. I found when I'm actively listening, my daughter is able to process her emotions more effectively and come up with solutions to problems. Even if she is having a bad day and responds out of anger, she comes back to apologize. Why? Because I lead by example by being transparent about my strengths and weaknesses. Researchers have also identified four types of communication styles: passive, passive-aggressive, aggressive, and assertive.

These styles contribute to healthy or unhealthy relationships, so it's important that we as parents know what these four styles are and which ones we operate in. Not knowing what these styles are and how they may be affecting communication in our home could be detrimental to the young people. So, let's take a brief look at the four styles of communication.

Passive Communicator: Don't Want to Offend

The passive style communicator often has a difficult time expressing their feelings or needs, because they don't like confrontation with others. This style of communicator may "beat around the bush" instead of telling people what they want: "I wish someone would remember to ask me what I want for my birthday," instead of telling the person they would like a certain gift for their birthday. Passive Communicators have suppressed emotions that may lead to unresolved anger, resentment, emotional instability, or unforgiveness. Research studies have shown suppressed emotions cause depression, anxiety, physical illnesses such as high blood pressure and low self-esteem.

Passive-Aggressive Communicator: Nice-Nasty

Passive-aggressive communicators have a difficult time expressing their feelings or needs because they want to avoid confrontation with others. However, due to suppressed anger, resentment, and unforgiveness, they act out in subtle or indirect ways.

The passive-aggressive communicator is aware of their needs; however, they go about it the wrong way, using deception and manipulation to get their point across. This type of communicator often acts out by giving people the silent treatment, guilt trip, or by playing on others' weakness. They tend to communicate using sarcasm, but in a joking manner, by gossiping and complaining behind people's back. Some will even sabotage others' efforts.

Aggressive Communicator: The Bully or Intimidator

The aggressive communicator is always heard and seen in a negative or fearful manner. They lack respect for others' opinions and advice. This style of communication is demanding and loud. Many times, their body language is intense, and they control the conversation by dominating others in the form of belittling, blame, and intimidation. The aggressive communicator will bark out commands, refuse to listen to others during the conversation, and rudely ask questions.

Assertive Communicator: Healthy Communicator

The assertive communicator can express their own needs, ideas, and feelings, while also considering the needs of others. This style of communication is found to be the most effective. It allows both sides to express their thoughts and feelings by using "I" statements, such as "I feel _____ because of _____" without placing blame, guilt, or shame on the other person.

Communication is one of the most fundamental

keys to any relationship, especially a parent-child relationship. The words we speak can bring edification to our children or death and destruction. The Bible says that "a soft answer turneth away wrath: but grievous words stir up anger," This is why it is extremely important to understand how our communication styles affect our children's ability to be honest about the world around them. Take an honest look at your communication style from a practical and biblical viewpoint.

Open-Ended Questions

After reviewing the four different communication styles, answer the questions below:

1. What communication style(s) do you resemble most? Why?

_____

_____

_____

_____

_____

_____

_____

_____

2. What communication style(s) did your parents

   have when you were growing up?

_____

_____

_____

_____

_____

_____

_____

_____

3. Did you adopt all or some of your parents'

   communication styles?

_____

_____

_____

_____

_____

_____

_____

_____

4. How did your parents influence your communication style?

_____

_____

_____

_____

_____

_____

_____

5. If you were to ask your children about your communication style, what do you think they would they say?

_____

_____

_____

_____

_____

_____

_____

_____

6. If married, how often do you communicate with your spouse? What style of communication is often used?

_____

_____

_____

_____

_____

_____

_____

_____

_____

7. If single, how often do you communicate with your child's mother or father? What style of communication is often used?

_____

_____

_____

_____

_____

_____

_____

_____

8. If a blended family, how often do you and your

spouse communicate with the children's mother or father? What style of communication is often used?

_____

_____

_____

_____

_____

_____

_____

_____

9. What communication style do(es) your child(ren) have?

_____

_____

_____

_____

_____

_____

_____

_____

_____

10. What are some barriers that are preventing

healthy communication in your household?

_____

_____

_____

_____

_____

_____

_____

_____

11. What are some strengths you have when

communicating with your children?

_____

_____

_____

_____

_____

_____

_____

_____

_____

Biblical Questions

God gives His pattern in the Bible for communicating. After reading the accompanying Scripture, answer the questions below in the space provided:

1. What does God say about what we speak?
   Proverbs 18:21; Matthew 12:36

_____

_____

_____

_____

_____

_____

_____

_____

_____

2. What does God say about listening? **James 1:19**

_____

_____

_____

_____

_____

_____

_____

_____

3. What does God say about how we should speak? **Colossians 4:6; Philippians 4:8; Roman 12:14-15**

_____

_____

_____

_____

_____

_____

_____

_____

4. What happens when we speak out of negative
   emotions? **Proverbs 18:13**

_____

_____

_____

_____

_____

_____

_____

5. What does God say about one-sided
   conversations? **Proverbs 18:2**

_____

_____

_____

_____

_____

_____

_____

_____

6. How does God help us to be slow to speak?
   Psalm 141:3; Psalm 19:14

_____

_____

_____

_____

_____

_____

_____

_____

_____

7. How does God instruct us to speak? **Psalm
   141:3; Psalm 19:14; Colossians 4:6**

_____

_____

_____

_____

_____

_____

_____

8. How does God instruct us to handle anger?
   Proverbs 15:1; Romans 12:14-15

_____

_____

_____

_____

_____

_____

_____

_____

_____

9. What does the Word of God say about how our thinking controls the way we speak? **Philippians 4:8; Matthew 12:34-37**

_____

_____

_____

_____

_____

_____

_____

_____

Reflection:

After answering the above questions, take the next 10 minutes to reflect on what you wrote from a practical and biblical viewpoint. This time of reflection is to raise your awareness about any old patterns, beliefs, and mindsets that may have created barriers of unhealthy communication within the household.

After your time of reflection, use the space provided below to journal about the following questions:

(1) What did you learn overall from answering the questions: positive and/or negative emotions, thoughts, and feelings?

_____

_____

_____

_____

_____

_____

_____

_____

_____

_____

_____

_____

_____

_____

_____

_____

(2) What communication style(s) did you most identify with? Why? Were you surprised?

_____

_____

_____

_____

_____

_____

_____

_____

_____

_____

_____

_____

_____

_____

_____

_____

(3) After learning more about your communication style(s), do you have to ask for forgiveness from yourself, your parents, your children, and/or others? If so, why?

_____

_____

_____

_____

_____

_____

_____

_____

_____

_____

_____

_____

_____

_____

_____

(4) How can the Word of God assist you in making

changes?

_____

_____

_____

_____

_____

_____

_____

_____

_____

_____

_____

_____

_____

_____

_____

_____

_____

_____

_____

(5) What strengths do you have that you can continue to implement as a healthy parent on a

consistent basis in your household?

_____

_____

_____

_____

_____

_____

_____

_____

_____

_____

_____

_____

_____

_____

_____

_____

_____

Chapter 3

Assess Your Atmosphere

"We wrestle not against flesh and blood, but against principalities, against powers, against rulers of the darkness of this world, against spiritual wickedness in high places" (Ephesians 6:12).

God had given us the greatest gift ever; children. As parents, we must accept responsibility when we miss the mark of effectively communicating with our children due to old beliefs, mindsets, religious traditions, and behaviors. This has caused a breach within the household. In order to repair the breach, you must first assess your current home atmosphere, especially now that you are able to identify barriers to communication from information you learned in previous chapters.

Let's take a closer look at what "atmosphere" means. An atmosphere is defined as "surrounding influences or environments" that determine how a home functions on a daily basis. As believers in Christ, we know we live in two atmospheres; the natural (physical) and the spiritual. The natural atmosphere is where we have our five senses: sight, smell, touch, hearing, and taste. The spiritual realm is something you can't see but know it is real. For example, have you ever walked into a room and sensed the atmosphere was not right, such as tension? Or you walked into a home, and you felt calmness or peace?

Atmospheres are important because the Bible tells us in Ephesians 6:12, "We wrestle not against flesh and blood, but against principalities, against powers, against the rulers of the darkness of this world, against spiritual wickedness in high places." So, we know we can't just live in the physical atmosphere and avoid the spiritual atmosphere, or vice versa. As parents, it's our responsibility to establish a home atmosphere that is nurturing, encouraging, and a safe place where the line of communication is open and free. It's also important to repent and ask for the blood of Jesus to cleanse and forgive us for any words spoken directly or indirectly from hurt, rejection, or tiredness that may have contributed to the atmosphere being unhealthy. Listed below you will have the opportunity to take an honest look at your home atmosphere by answering questions from a practical and biblical viewpoint.

Open-Ended Questions

Answer the questions below in the space provided regarding your current home atmosphere:

1. As you reflect back over the last two weeks, what does a typical day in your family household look like? Is the atmosphere peaceful, chaotic,

vexing, competitive, etc.?

_____

_____

_____

_____

_____

_____

_____

_____

2. How often does the household pray together?

_____

_____

_____

_____

_____

_____

_____

3. How often does the household study the Word
    of God together?

    _____

    _____

    _____

    _____

    _____

    _____

    _____

    _____

4. Does your family go to church together?

    _____

    _____

    _____

    _____

    _____

    _____

_____

_____

_____

5. How often does your family come together for family activities?

_____

_____

_____

_____

_____

_____

_____

_____

6. If married, how often do you and your spouse communicate?

_____

_____

_____

_____

_____

_____

_____

_____

7. If single, do you have a support system you communicate with?

_____

_____

_____

_____

_____

_____

_____

_____

8. How often does the household come together to communicate (family meetings)?

_____

_____

_____

_____

_____

_____

_____

_____

9. How often does the family come together to discuss questions or concerns?

_____

_____

_____

_____

_____

_____

_____

_____

10. How does the household communicate their needs and wants?

_____

_____

_____

_____

_____

_____

_____

_____

11. How often does each child talk about accomplishments? Struggles?

_____

_____

_____

_____

_____

_____

_____

_____

_____

12. What are the gifts and talents of everyone in the household?

_____

_____

_____

_____

_____

_____

_____

_____

13. Based on the gifts and talents of everyone, how do you meet the needs of everyone?

_____

_____

_____

_____

_____

_____

_____

_____

_____

14. How often is praise and encouragement given?

_____

_____

_____

_____

_____

_____

_____

_____

15. Is there any dissension amongst the family? If so, what? Why?

_____

_____

_____

_____

_____

_____

_____

_____

_____

16. Does anyone suffer from any medical conditions, mental health diagnosis, or addictions?

_____

_____

_____

_____

_____

_____

_____

_____

_____

17. How does it affect how you communicate with

self? Others? Children?

_____

_____

_____

_____

_____

_____

_____

_____

18. Do you have a loved one currently incarcerated

or involved with the criminal justice system?

_____

_____

_____

_____

_____

_____

_____

_____

_____

19. If yes to question 18, how does it affect how you communicate with self? Others? Your children?

_____

_____

_____

_____

_____

_____

_____

_____

Biblical Questions

God gives His pattern in the Bible for unity. After reading the accompanying Scripture, answer the questions below in the space provided:

1. What does God say about unity? **1 Corinthians 1:10; Colossians 3:13-14; John 17:23; Psalm 133:1; Ephesians 4:3; Roman 12:4; Amos 3:3**

_____

_____

_____

_____

_____

_____

_____

_____

2. What does God say about family operating as a unit? **Ephesians 4:11-13; Ephesians 4:16; 1 Corinthians 12:12-13**

_____

_____

_____

_____

_____

_____

_____

_____

3. What does God say about walking in love? **1 Peter 3:8; 1 John 4:12; Philippians 2:1**

_____

_____

_____

_____

_____

_____

_____

_____

4. What does God say about peace in the household? **Romans 12:16; Ephesians 2:14**

_____

_____

_____

_____

_____

_____

_____

_____

Reflection:

After answering the above questions, take the next 10 minutes to reflect on what you wrote from a practical and biblical viewpoint. This time of reflection is to raise your awareness about any old patterns, beliefs, and mindsets that may have created barriers of unhealthy communication within the household.

After your time of reflection, use the space provided below to journal about the following questions:

(1) What did you learn overall from answering the questions: positive and/or negative emotions, thoughts, and feelings?

_____

_____

_____

_____

_____

_____

_____

_____

_____

_____

_____

_____

_____

_____

_____

_____

_____

(2) What did you learn about your current home

atmosphere?

_____

_____

_____

_____

_____

_____

_____

_____

_____

_____

_____

_____

_____

_____

_____

_____

_____

(3) How can the Word of God assist you in making

changes?

_____

_____

_____

_____

_____

_____

_____

_____

_____

_____

_____

_____

_____

_____

_____

_____

_____

(4) What strengths does your household have that
    you can continue to implement for a healthy
    home atmosphere?

_____

_____

_____

_____

_____

_____

_____

_____

_____

_____

_____

_____

_____

_____

_____

_____

_____

Chapter 4

Command Your Atmosphere

"Death and Life are in the power of the tongue: and they that love it shall eat the fruit thereof" (Proverbs 18:21).

As you read and answered the questions in the previous chapters, you were able to identify specific barriers in your current atmosphere that are preventing healthy communication within your household, especially with your children.

As Christian parents, we have the authority to command the Word of God to operate within our homes. Our words are so powerful that they can promote peace or chaos. The Bible tells us death and life are in the power of the tongue. It's very important that we understand that the words we speak are edifying and provide significant influence of how our kids act and view themselves.

The word *command* is defined as "to give an authoritative order." In the book of Genesis chapter 1, God spoke to the darkness and commanded the light to come forth. So, when you speak the Word of God, the atmosphere has no choice but to obey. We have the authority given by God to speak the Word of God by faith and command our atmosphere to align with the Will of God. Hebrew 4:12 says, "The Word of God is quick, and powerful, and sharper than any two-edged sword, piercing even to the dividing asunder of soul and spirit, and if the joints and marrow, and is a discerner of the thoughts and intents of the heart."

Satan knows if families are walking on one accord, the kingdom of darkness is in trouble. He knows the Word of God drives out darkness. Therefore, if families walk in the original plan to have dominion and walk in their God-given authority, he will have no legal right to continue to inflict death and destruction for generations to come. This is why the adversary does his best to create barriers such as confusion, deception, and misunderstanding to stop healthy communication within the household.

Speaking the Word of God can break every scheme of the enemy that will hinder healthy communication in the household. You have the power to take authority over every barrier that comes against what God has said regarding you and your household. It is to your advantage to use the Word of God to command your atmosphere to be healthy by making declarations and decrees.

By faith, declare and decree that the words your household speaks have authority to change every atmosphere that is not like God. By faith, declare and decree that healthy communication is your family's portion. By faith, declare and decree that your household is speaking words that are promoting life, unity, peace, and joy. By faith, declare and decree that every word spoken within the household is aligned to God's purposes and plans. YOU have the power within YOU! Speak, believe, and receive it!

Four Week Declaration and Journal Challenge

As you read earlier in this chapter, we have the power and authority to speak the Word of God and command our home atmosphere to align with the purposes and plans of God. Listed below are a series of instructions for you to begin the process of changing your home atmosphere with the words you speak, and have the opportunity over the next four weeks to journal the experience.

Before you begin journaling, go back to chapters one through three and review your responses in the reflection section. Once you have reviewed the reflection sections, please follow the instructions below:

1. Identify and write down the top 2-3 areas of concerns that you need to improve upon in your household. Why did you choose these areas? What are you looking to gain by addressing these areas of concern?

_____

_____

_____

_____

_____

_____

_____

_____

_____

_____

_____

_____

_____

_____

_____

_____

_____

2. For the areas of concerns identified in #1, look in your Bible or Google 3-5 scriptures that deal with that problem. For example, if your area of concern is anger, you would find scriptures that deal with peace, self-control, and responding in love.

_____

_____

_____

_____

_____

_____

_____

_____

_____

_____

_____

_____

_____

_____

_____

_____

3. Now that you were able to identify areas of concern and scriptures, for the next four weeks, begin to speak, declare, and decree the scriptures identified in #2 every morning and evening. For example, "Lord, your Word says_____, and I declare and decree that your Word is true and is changing my home

atmosphere to bring unity, peace, and love in my household."

_____

_____

_____

_____

_____

_____

_____

_____

_____

_____

_____

_____

_____

_____

4. As you begin to speak and pray the scriptures on a daily basis, don't forget to include journaling as well. Journal daily your thoughts, feelings, attitude, and any prayer requests you are seeking from the Lord. You may need additional writing paper if you run out of space provided in this guide. Throughout the journaling process, if you need help collecting your thoughts, ask yourself a few questions to aid you in what to write to help command your atmosphere. Did you notice a positive shift in the atmosphere by speaking the Word of God? Family? Self? Did you face any challenges? If so, how did you respond? Did your faith and trust increase?

_____

_____

_____

_____

_____

_____

_____

_____

_____

_____

_____

_____

_____

_____

_____

_____

_____

You may find long after you finish reading this guide that you enjoy the journaling process and want to continue using it as a tool. You may even opt to encourage family members to journal. Journaling is a great tool and resource to sort out your thoughts, feelings, attitude, prayer requests, track personal progress or growth and more.

Chapter 5

Create Your Atmosphere

"Through wisdom is an house builded; and by understanding it is established: And by knowledge shall the chambers be filled with all precious and pleasant riches" (Proverbs 24:3-4).

Parents have the responsibility to create a positive atmosphere that fosters a safe, nurturing and loving place where the lines of communication are open. In Matthew 19: 13-15, Jesus is the greatest example. He created an atmosphere where children were comfortable enough to sit and talk with him. This example shows us how we are to be with our children. The children recognized Jesus with authority. The atmosphere changed simply by Jesus speaking and laying hands on them. Shouldn't our own children be able to come to us, recognizing that we carry that same type of authority within us; to speak life, blessings, hope, and power to change every circumstance and situation? Yes, our children should see Christ within us!

In Genesis 1: 26, God created man in His image to be fruitful, to multiply, replenish the earth and subdue it; and have dominion. As parents, we have the role to create an atmosphere in the home that is fruitful and multiplying by producing healthy communication that results in unity, love, joy, and peace.

Listed below are some tips on how you can begin to strategically develop a plan of action to create an atmosphere for healthy communication:

1. Create a mission statement for your home. Write the vision and make it plain (Habakkuk 2:2). What do you want to happen in your

household (see sample in "Additional Resources" section)?

2. Set guidelines and boundaries on how to communicate; no yelling; use "I" statements, such as "I feel" without placing the blame, shame, or guilt on the other person.

3. Ask your children their opinion about the family including likes, dislikes, and ways to improve communication.

4. Show humility. Ask for forgiveness and simply say, "I'm sorry." Don't be judgmental.

5. Set aside time to talk (in the car, at dinner, shopping, etc.). Be intentional.

6. Set aside time for weekly Bible study in a specific meeting place.

7. Set aside time to worship, praise, and play music that is uplifting.

8. Set aside time to pray daily (individually and collectively).

9. Find out each member's strength, gifts, and talents.

10. As a household, create family declarations and decrees to speak daily or on a weekly basis.

11. As a household, create family outings; times spent having fun, and time relaxing (not on smart devices or social media). If you have more than one child, make time to spend with each child alone.

12. Seek counseling or coaching if needed.

Healthy communication is an essential key to building unity in the household. Commanding or speaking the Word of God brings power to change any atmosphere that doesn't line up with God promises. God's promises are "yes" and "amen." Creating an atmosphere that promotes open communication closes the door to the enemy to come in and bring separation, discord, and confusion. God wants his families displaying who He is on this earth.

Additional Resources

Sample Mission Statement:

Our home is committed to being a representation of the Lord by creating an atmosphere that is conducive to speaking life, love, peace, and unity.

For the free downloads *"3 Tips to Improve Communications in the Parent-Child Relationship"* and *"5 Tips to Deal with Teenage Rebellion,"* visit www. befreeandspeak.com or www.candicepsimpson.com.

To purchase *Mom!!!Really???: A Faith-Based Guide for Parents to Engage in Healthy Conversation Starters with Their Youth and Young Adults*, visit www. befreeandspeak.com or www.candicepsimpson.com.

Join Us on Social Media! Facebook, Twitter, and Instagram @momreally

About the Author

Candice P. Simpson, PhD is the CEO and founder of Be Free Enterprises, LLC. Be Free Enterprises is a coaching and consultant company dedicated to the advancement and development of people to fulfill their God-given purpose and destiny.

Candice is an experienced life coach, addiction counselor, and speaker. She has her Doctorate degree in Theology and is an Ordained Minister. She infuses the application of God's principles found in His Word by being transparent, straightforward, and applying strategic techniques. She knows it is the pure, unchanging, unlimited Word of God that will save, heal, and set the people free.

Candice is also a Licensed Independent Chemical Dependency Counselor. She obtained her Master's

Degree in Criminal Justice Administration. She has more than 12 years of experience in the criminal justice field. Her knowledge of the prison system, faith-based communities, and state agencies provides her with the essential tools to uniquely benefit individuals and organization.

Candice owes her success to her daughter. Being a single parent has taught her five key principles in life: (1) pray without ceasing, (2) maintain healthy communication, (3) stay disciplined, (4) be consistent and (5) lead by example.

You can learn more about Candice by visiting her at www.candicepsimpson.com or www.befreeandspeak.com.

<u>NOTES</u>

<u>NOTES</u>

<u>NOTES</u>

<u>NOTES</u>

<u>NOTES</u>

<u>NOTES</u>

<u>NOTES</u>

<u>NOTES</u>

<u>NOTES</u>

<u>NOTES</u>